THIS BOOK WAS WRITTEN & ILLUSTRATED BY
CHRIS SABATINO, A GUY WHO HAS LIVED IN
AND AROUND THE BOSTON AREA ALL HIS LIFE!

city doodles
BOSTON

CHRIS SABATINO

GIBBS SMITH
TO ENRICH AND INSPIRE HUMANKIND

Manufactured in Altona, Manitoba, Canada,
in February 2013 by Friesens

First Edition
17 16 15 14 13   5 4 3 2 1

Published by
Gibbs Smith
P.O. Box 667
Layton, Utah 84041

1.800.835.4993 orders
www.gibbs-smith.com

Designed by Melissa Dymock

Gibbs Smith books are printed on either
recycled, 100% post-consumer waste, FSC-
certified papers or on paper produced from
sustainable PEFC-certified forest/controlled
wood source. Learn more at www.pefc.org.

ISBN 13: 978-1-4236-3207-8

Over 600,000 people live in Boston. Draw yourself entering this amazing city.

Boston has crazy weather. Draw a sun, some clouds, snowflakes, and a few raindrops around this Boston fisherman.

Boston loves its sports teams. Draw the four different sports these Boston fans are watching at the same time.

Boston is known for its great food from both land and sea. What has this chef prepared for dinner?

There's history and art around every corner in Boston. Draw your teacher's excited face.

Boston is a leader in medicine, science, and education. What are these smart Bostonians thinking about?

People in Boston have their own accent. Try to figure out what this Bostonian is saying.

WHAT DID HE SAY? (THERE IS NO WRONG ANSWER)

I Parked my car at the corner and caught the Red Sox at the park

Faneuil Hall has a golden grasshopper weathervane on its roof. Finish drawing it.

These musicians are welcoming
you to the marketplace.
Give them some instruments.

What is this vendor selling
on her pushcart?

FANEUIL HALL
MARKETPLACE

In Quincy Market you can
get all kinds of great food.
Draw what you'd like to eat.

The crowd is enjoying a street performer outside Quincy Market. Draw their expressions.

The caricaturist is creating
a portrait of you.
Doodle your face.

Draw the funny objects this performer is juggling.

The magician is pulling something
very strange from his hat.

Who's sharing a soda?

Cover this ice cream with all your favorite toppings.
(No Boston baked beans please!)

Faneuil Hall's nickname is "The Cradle of Liberty." Draw a baby American Eagle in his cradle.

Draw the bunch of balloons lifting this mime above Faneuil Hall and Quincy Market.

Faneuil Hall was originally a meeting place. Draw someone you'd like to meet there.

The Red Sox have had many different uniforms. Design a new uniform.

The Fenway Frank is the delicious
hot dog served at Fenway Park.
What do you like on yours?

The Green Monster is the giant scoreboard in Fenway Park. What is the Yankees player doodling on the wall?

Wally the Green Monster is the Sox's mascot. Create a monster for Wally to play catch with.

Who or what is this foul ball
about to hit at Fenway Park?

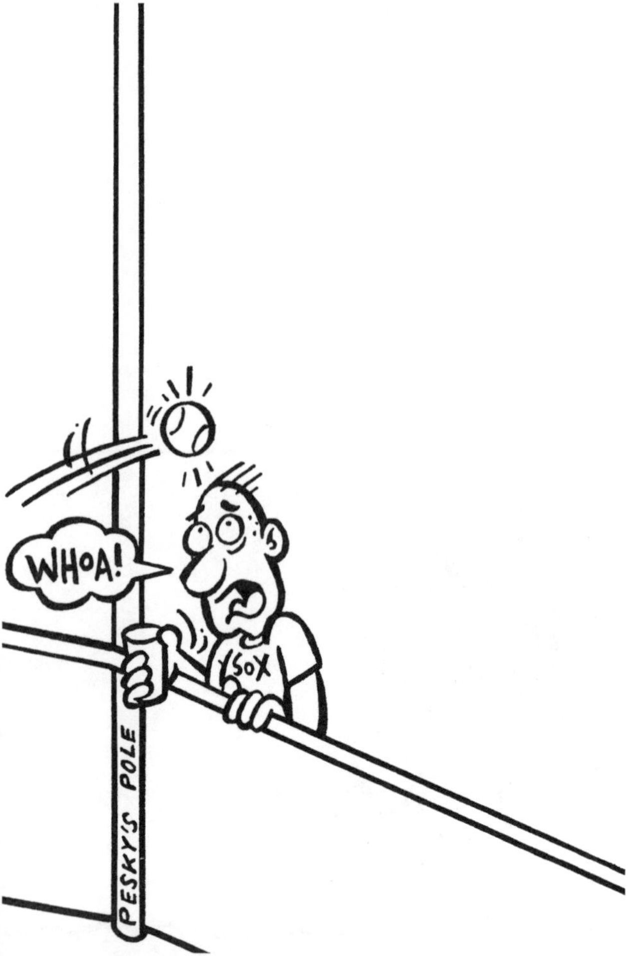

Draw a friend or family member on the pitcher's mound who would love to pitch for the Red Sox.

Doodle the weird object this Red
Sox player is using as a bat.

Draw a real bat working as the Red Sox bat boy.

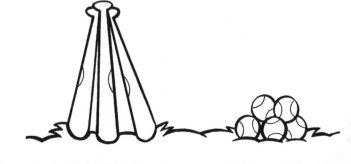

What are the umpire and the
catcher arguing about?

The large CITGO sign overlooking Fenway Park is now a historical landmark. What is this Sox fan thinking?

Like the old woman who lived in a shoe, this Red Sox player lives in a giant red sock. Draw it.

Decorate her clothing and give her some souvenirs to make this lady the ultimate Sox fan.

Fenway Park just celebrated its 100th birthday! How would you decorate a cake for a ballpark?

At first, cows and sheep grazed in Boston Common. Draw a cow having a picnic with this sheep.

What would you bring on a picnic to Boston Common?

Every year the Boston Common displays a huge Christmas tree. Give this one some decorations.

Build a snowman in the Common.

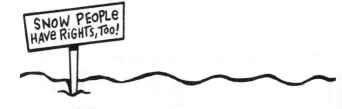

Who's taking a nice cool refreshing swim in Boston Common's Frog Pond?

It's wintertime at Boston Common.
Who's skating some figure eights
on the ice covered Frog Pond?

These instruments are late for a concert
at the Boston Common bandstand.
Who or what else is also late?

Boston Common has great areas
for softball, tennis, and Frisbee.
What just hit this guy on the head?

Boston Common is a great place to walk your dog. Draw the huge dog she's walking.

Draw the human this dog is
walking in the Common.

Shakespeare plays are often performed in Boston Common. Draw the squirrel playing Juliet.

The Boston Common is the site
of the beautiful Brewer Fountain.
Design your own fountain.

There's an old cemetery within
the Boston Common.
Draw the ghost of a patriot.

Destroyed by a storm in 1876, the
Great Elm Tree in Boston Common
was the site of public hangings.
Play a game of hangman with a friend.

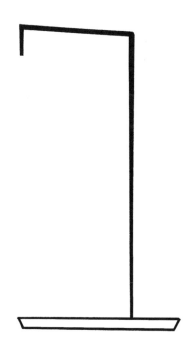

Draw how you'd like to spend a day in Boston Common.

In front of the Boston Children's
Museum there's a 40-foot
high milk bottle. Draw it.

The Boston Children's Museum has hands-on exhibits that will excite your mind. Draw her excited brain.

Boston's Museum of Fine Arts opened in 1876 and displays amazing artwork. Draw something beautiful.

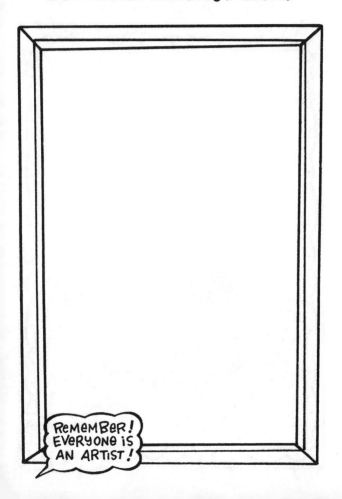

Boston's Museum of Bad Art opened in 1993 and brings the worst of art to Boston. Draw something ugly.

Draw what you'd see at
the planetarium in Boston's
Museum of Science.

The MIT (Massachusetts Institute of Technology) Museum is all about ideas and inventions. Create a robot tour guide.

Learn Boston's sports history at the
Sport's Museum in the TD Garden.
Draw your favorite Boston athlete.

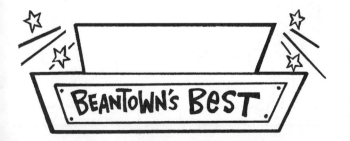

The John F. Kennedy Presidential Library and Museum was built in honor of our 35th President. Create your campaign poster.

In 1990 thieves stole famous artwork from Boston's Isabella Stewart Gardner Museum. Who's sneaking away with this painting?

Draw yourself as an early colonist on Boston's Freedom Trail.

Draw some of the friendly birds you're likely to see in Boston Common on the Freedom Trail.

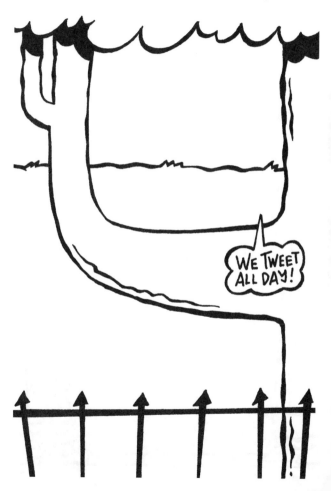

Add the shiny gold dome on top of the Massachusetts State House.

Draw the American Flag hanging from the Old State House Museum.

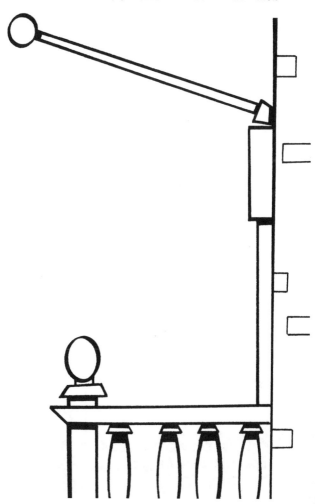

There's a statue of Benjamin
Franklin along the Freedom Trail.
Draw Ben flying his kite.

Boston's Freedom Trail passes by Paul Revere's house. Draw Paul mowing his lawn.

Draw two lanterns hanging in the window of the Old North Church.

Design and draw a steeple for King's Chapel.

The Boston Massacre started as an argument between Bostonians and the British. What do you think they said?

Time to rest and have a
snack at Faneuil Hall.
Draw your favorite snack.

FANEUIL HALL ON
THE FREEDOM TRAIL

Draw an angel outside the Park Street Church.

There are three graveyards on the Freedom Trail. What historical Bostonian is buried here?

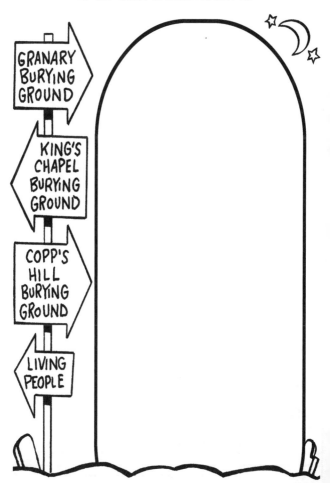

The Old Corner Bookstore was
built in 1711. Illustrate a page
from your favorite book.

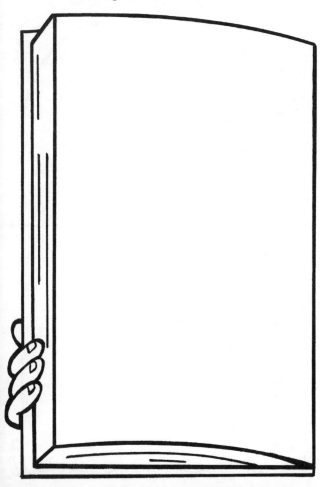

The Old South Meeting House was the
meeting place for the patriots called
the Sons of Liberty. Draw them.

Bunker Hill Monument was built in 1827 and is 221 feet high. What do you think the view looks like from the top?

FREEDOM TRAIL

The Battle of Bunker Hill took place in 1775. Draw a battle between the Redcoats and Colonial Troops.

On the Freedom Trail you'll find the warship USS Constitution, also known as Old Ironsides. Add some sails to her masts.

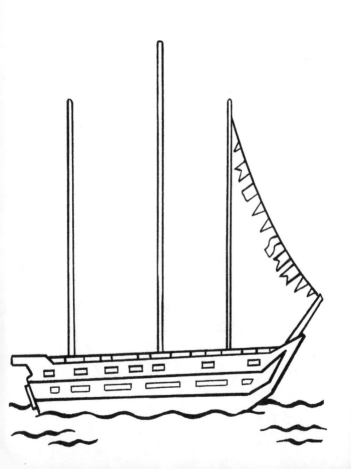

Draw one of your family members as
the captain of the USS Constitution.

Give these toes some very sad faces after their long walk on Boston's Freedom Trail.

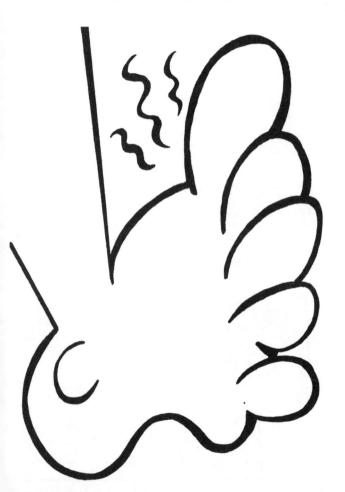

Some people get lost on the Freedom Trail. Draw some flying monkeys over Boston.

What part of Boston's Freedom
Trail did you enjoy the most?

Blades the Bear is the Boston
Bruins' mascot. Draw where
you think Blades lives.

The Stanley Cup is the trophy given for the best hockey team. What's jumping out of it?

During the playoff season, most
of the Boston Bruins grow beards.
Doodle a beard on this Bruin.

Draw someone you know hanging out in the Boston Bruins penalty box at the TD Garden.

Create a new goalie for the Boston Bruins that's so big no one will ever get a puck in the goal.

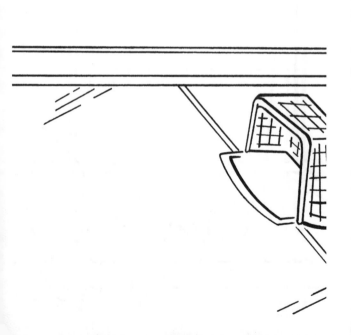

What's written on the signs the fans
at the TD Garden are holding?

Draw the giant this Celtics player is up against.

Lucky the Leprechaun is the Celtics' mascot. What has he magically made appear on the basketball court?

What is your favorite food to munch on during a Boston Celtics' game at the TD Garden?

Draw the silly object being thrown through the basket at the Celtics' game.

It's raining sporting equipment down on these fans in the TD Garden's Sports Museum.

Draw your favorite singer performing in concert at the TD Garden.

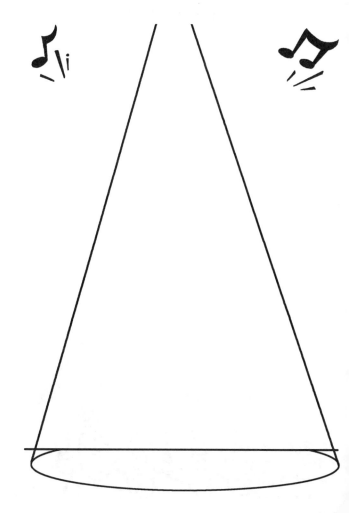

Draw an ice skating fish wearing a Red Sox hat, and juggling Boston baked beans in this ice show.

The circus is at the TD Garden.
Draw the clown's face that's about
to be hit by this Boston cream pie.

What are the Bruins' puck and the Celtics' ball arguing about at the TD Garden?

Draw a big smiling sun over
the Public Garden Bridge.

The Public Garden is full of plant life.
Draw a giant, friendly flower.

Draw your family taking a ride on the swan boats at the Public Garden.

At the back of each swan boat
is a big swan. Draw the swan.

In the Public Garden there's a
statue of George Washington riding
his horse. Draw George's horse.

There are many statues and
monuments in the Public Garden.
Create a statue of someone
special in your life.

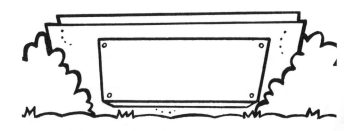

Make Way for Ducklings, written by Robert McCloskey takes place in the Public Garden, where there are statues of Mrs. Mallard and her ducklings. Draw the eight ducklings.

The eight ducklings are named
Jack, Kack, Lack, Mack, Nack,
Ouack, Pack, and Quack.

The Public Garden has many kinds of trees. Draw how this tree would look during Boston's four seasons.

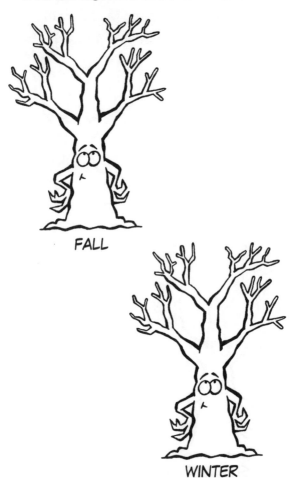

FALL

WINTER

SPRING

SUMMER

This boy is flying the weirdest kite ever. Draw it.

HUMANS LOVE TO FLY CRAZY THINGS IN BOSTON!

Who's singing on stage at the Boston Opera House?

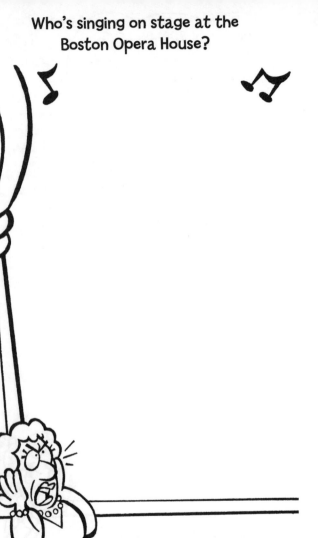

Draw the ballerina performing
for the Boston Ballet.

The Boston Symphony Orchestra
has been entertaining since 1881.
Draw this musician's harp.

Boston is the home of many rock bands like Aerosmith. Give this musician some drums.

Many famous writers, including Dr. Seuss are from Boston. Draw the cover of your favorite Dr. Seuss book.

The Boston Public Library
opened way back in 1848.
Draw a 150-year-old librarian.

Boston has many theaters.
What is everyone laughing at
in the Wilbur Theatre?

Put your name up in lights as the starring performer at the Colonial Theatre.

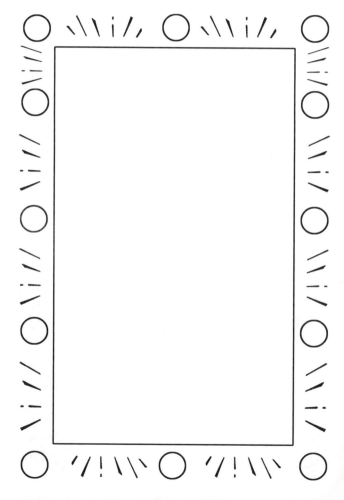

The Boston Pops Orchestra has had some famous conductors. Draw your Pop conducting the Boston Pops.

The Boston Pops sometimes perform
at the Hatch Shell, a shell-like stage.
Who's performing there tonight?

Draw the musical notes flying out of the windows of Boston's Berklee College of Music.

Boston has many art schools like the New England School of Art & Design. Draw this student's artwork.

A concert? A play? A comedian?
Draw what you'd love to
see on stage in Boston.

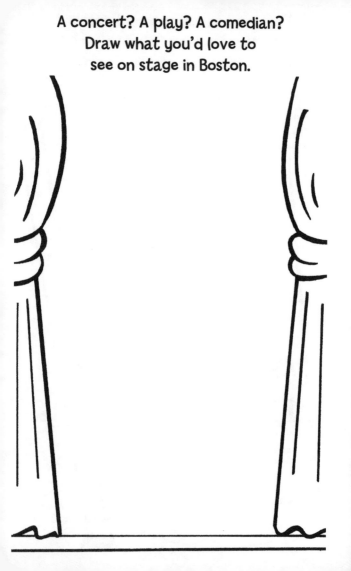

Many fans at Gillette Stadium paint their faces. How would you paint this fan's face for a Patriots' game?

The Patriots' mascot, Pat Patriot, is late for a game. Create a football shaped car to get him to Gillette Stadium.

Who or what are Patriot cheerleaders throwing in the air?

What kind of goodies is this vendor selling at the Patriots' football game?

Doodle something funny on the giant video screen at Gillette Stadium.

A football is also called a pigskin.
Draw a pig marrying this football.

What did someone doodle on the back of this New England Patriots player's jersey?

What is the mascot for the New England Revolution soccer team holding up to get the crowd excited?

What is this Revolution player kicking by accident?

The New England Revolution hired Bigfoot to be their goalie. Draw him in front of the soccer goal.

Create a tattoo on the arm
of this soccer fan.

The soccer ball at Gillette Stadium finally gets a chance to kick something. Draw it.

The Boston Tea Party.
Draw the colonists rebelling against
the British in 1773 by dumping
tea into Boston Harbor.

IMPORTED
TEA

Draw Paul Revere making his famous midnight ride to warn the colonists that the British were coming to attack in 1775.

It's March 17, 1776, the end of the Siege of Boston and the beginning of the American Revolutionary War. Draw Bostonians celebrating as the British are finally leaving their city.

Draw some of the tired runners competing in the Boston Marathon; the world's oldest 26-mile marathon that started in 1879.

Draw who you'd like to win
the Boston Marathon.

Commonly referred to as "The Blizzard of '78," when 27 inches of snow fell on Boston in February of that year; what would you do in all that snow?

The Big Dig.
Draw something scary they may
have dug up when moving Boston's
main highway into a tunnel.

Draw the ice sculpture this artist
is creating for Boston's New
Year's Eve festival, First Night.

Doodle the July 4th fireworks going off over the Charles River as the Boston Pops play at the Hatch Shell.

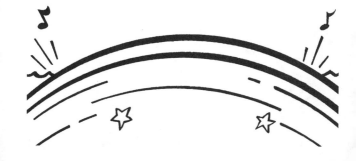

Create a wild float for South Boston's annual St. Patrick's Day parade.

The Feast of St. Anthony is celebrated every August in Boston's North End. What yummy food are you looking forward to eating at the feast?

Draw one of the dancing toy soldiers
performing in *The Nutcracker*,
an annual holiday event staged
by the Boston Ballet.

PEANUTS HATE THIS SHOW!

The Scooper Bowl.
Fill these cones with all your
favorite flavors at Boston's all-
you-can-eat ice cream festival.

Draw a historical event in your life.

Many visitors who come to
Boston arrive at Logan Airport.
Draw all the planes flying over Logan.

People say that Boston is famous for its traffic jams. Draw the expression on the face of this driver stuck in traffic.

It's not really true that there are a
lot of bad drivers in Boston, but draw
the strange object this Bostonian hit.

Boston has many buses, trains, and a subway. Draw some more crazy characters on this crowded subway car.

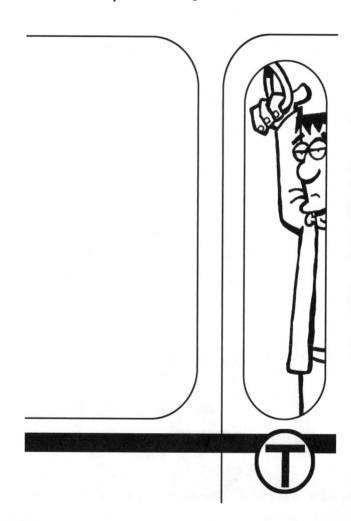

Help Logan get through this maze of the city to the Prudential Building so he can enjoy a sky-high view of Boston.

A great way to get around Boston is by bike. Who's joining you for a ride on this bicycle built for five?

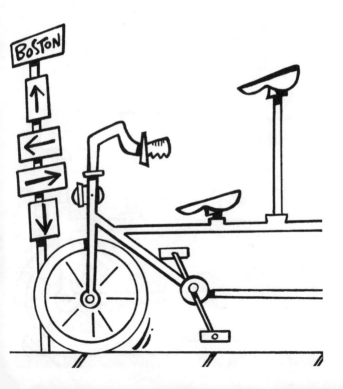

The best way to get around Boston is on foot. Draw a different shoe for every leg of this lost octopus.

How would you travel around Boston during a blizzard?

Boston Duck Boats can travel on both land and water. Draw a group of ducks on the Boston Duck Tour.

ARE YOU GOING TO TAKE MANY PHOTOS?
ONE IF BY LAND AND TWO IF BY SEA!
THIS IS BETTER THAN FLYING SOUTH!
YOU GUYS QUACK ME UP!
BOSTON • DUCK • TOURS
LAND & WATER

Draw yourself as a superhero flying over Boston.

What is this very lost visitor asking at the information booth?

Doodle the way you'd like to
travel around Boston.

Draw some of the undersea
creatures you've discovered in
the Giant Ocean Tank at Boston's
New England Aquarium.

More than 80 Penguins live at
the New England Aquarium.
Fill this exhibit with penguins.

Draw the two real lovebirds in this horse drawn carriage going through Boston Common.

What kind of critter has this Boston Animal Control Officer captured?

Draw your favorite animal living at Boston's Franklin Park Zoo.

This dentist is checking the teeth of a crocodile at the Franklin Park Zoo. Draw the crocodile's big mouth.

Create the peanut butter fish hanging with this jellyfish in Boston Harbor.

Draw the giant pigeon that's chasing this girl through Boston's Public Garden.

Draw the people enjoying
this Boston whale watch.

Draw a whale!

A famous Boston bird is Larry Bird,
who played for the Boston Celtics.
Draw a bird playing basketball.

Draw the animal that this
Boston Terrier is boxing with.

Draw a messy Bostonian eating at this all-you-can-eat Boston seafood buffet.

In the year 1620, the Mayflower landed
at Plymouth Rock in Plymouth.
Draw some of the Pilgrims
who made that journey.

What do you think the Pilgrims
served at the first Thanksgiving?
Draw their feast.

The spooky town of Salem is known for its witch trials in 1692. What's flying over the Salem Witch Museum?

Draw the ghost hanging
around outside The House of
The Seven Gables in Salem.

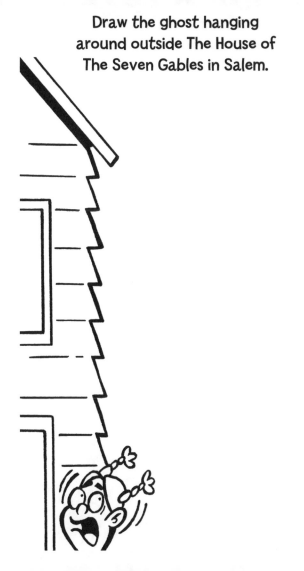

Fig Newtons are cookies named
after the town of Newton.
Draw your favorite cookie.

Waltham is also known as "Watch City." Draw a face on this living watch made in Waltham.

Johnny Appleseed was born in Leominster. Draw the giant worm he's arguing with.

Basketball was born in Springfield.
Who is this baby playing
basketball with?

Draw the tree being hugged by writer Henry David Thoreau, who lived by Walden Pond near Concord.

In 1801, Paul Revere moved to Canton
and started making steeple bells.
Draw a large Revere bell.

Draw the silly mermaid who's fallen in love with the famous Fisherman's Memorial statue in Gloucester.

Draw the prize-winning pumpkin
at the giant pumpkin contest held
during the Topsfield Fair in Topsfield.

TOPSFIELD
FAIR

Doodle something that's special about your hometown.

How many suitcases has this family loaded on top of the car for their vacation on Cape Cod?

SHEiLA SELLS
SeASHeLLS BY
THe SeASHORe

Draw all the seashells she's
selling at the beach.

How many sunbathers have crowded this Cape Cod beach?

Cape Cod has many lighthouses.
Draw a lighthouse on the shore.

Draw a boat sailing around the bay.

Draw the hidden treasures you've found in the shop window.

You ate way too much saltwater taffy today. Draw the mini taffy monster in your stomach.

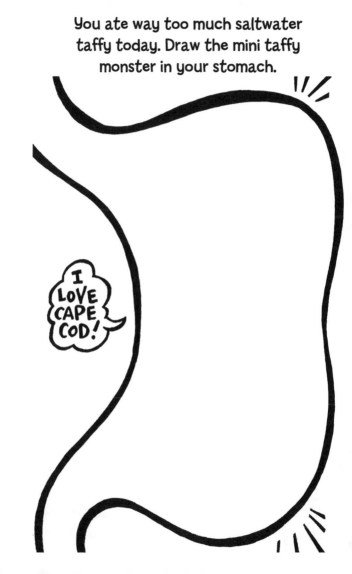

Draw the big fish he just reeled in.

What has this snorkeler discovered
in the waters of Cape Cod?

EEK! The movie "Jaws" was filmed around Cape Cod. Draw a shark about to surprise this lady.

Build an award-winning sandcastle.

What did you accidently hit with a
golf ball while playing miniature golf?

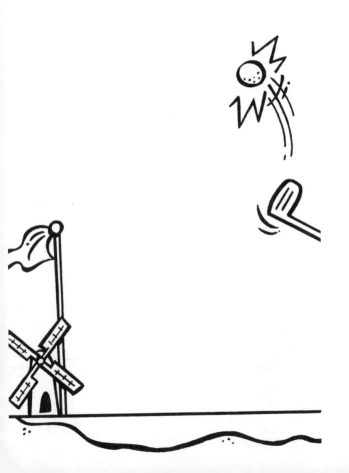

Create the Cape Cod Crusader, a superhero that protects Cape Cod.

Biking? Swimming? Shopping? Exploring? Draw how you'd like to spend a day on Cape Cod.

WE'VE SEEN SOME AMAZING THINGS DURING OUR DOODLE ADVENTURE THROUGH BOSTON! NOW LET'S CHECK OUT SOME OF THE "ODDS AND ENDS" OF BOSTON THAT YOU MIGHT FIND INTERESTING AS WELL!
B
B
DOODLE THE CANNON I'M BEING SHOT OUT OF AS I SOAR OVER MY HOMETOWN OF BOSTON!

A 227 gallon tea kettle hangs in Boston on Court Street. Draw the giant hanging tea kettle.

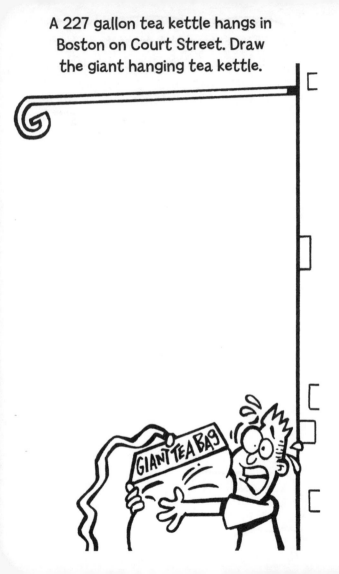

1919's Great Molasses Flood happened when a molasses storage tank burst. Draw a scary molasses monster.

The first UFO sighting was in 1639, when several people reported seeing bright lights over the Charles River in Boston. Draw a spaceship over Boston.

THE MARTIANS
ARE COMING!
THE MARTIANS
ARE COMING!

ONE IF BY LAND,
TWO IF BY SEA,
THREE IF BY
OUTER SPACE!

The Nahant Sea Serpent has had reported sightings off the New England coast since the 1800s. Draw a sea monster in the Boston waters.

GREAT! ANOTHER GREEN MONSTER IN BOSTON!

The lights on top of the Berkeley Building forecast Boston's weather. Color the light and draw today's weather.

The biggest artwork in Boston is the rainbow design on the waterfront gas tank. What would you paint on the tank?

There are over thirty islands
in Boston Harbor. Draw who's
hanging out on Nut Island.

Castle Island and other Boston
islands have old forts on them.
Draw an awesome fort on this island.

Boston has many colleges and universities. Draw the huge stack of books this college student is carrying.

Boston's Harvard University is the oldest university in the United States. Draw a smart person who belongs at Harvard.

A professor at Boston's MIT created a robot with emotions named "Kismet." Can you create your own emotional robot?

What could colonial inventor Ben Franklin and this modern Boston scientist be talking about?

One of the world's thinnest houses is Boston's, The Skinny House. Draw a tall, thin family that could live in it.

Draw a giant crab on the top
of the John Hancock Tower, the
tallest building in Boston.

Draw how you think Boston will
look far into the future.

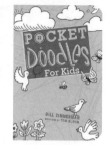

Collect Them All!

Available at bookstores or
directly from Gibbs Smith

1.800.835.4993

www.pocketdoodles.com